Fiery Pines

Written by P.A. Lin

Illustrated by V.A. Kitsco

Dedicated to Roger

Jack pines, jack pines, all around.
Your beauty truly does abound!

Your needles point up to the sky,
As you grow up really high.

What makes you really special, though,
Is your most amazing pinecones.

Filled with resin, those cones will sleep
'Til fire comes and seeds do seep
Into the ground to grow up tall
'Til fire comes and makes them fall.

Those cones do have a special name:
"Serotinous" cones, no two the same.
They cannot open without heat,
Which really, truly is quite neat!

The cones are held together, like glue,
Which only the heat of fire can undo.

After a fire, two million seeds
In an acre of land start growing like weeds.

When the jack pines are young, and close to the ground,
Within them the nests of Kirtland Warblers can be found.

Next time you are near to a jack pine tree,
Pick a cone and try to set the seeds free.

You'll see that it's impossible to do
Because of that strong, resinous glue.
The cone is as hard as a piece of iron ore,
Without fire the seeds just cannot soar.

iron ore

Every tree has something about it that's unique and quite grand.
The cones of Jack Pines won't open without fire on the land.

JACK PINE
tamarack
birch

So take a close look when you're out on a hike,
At the amazing jack pines that we all really like!

Fiery Pines
Word Search

```
S E E P L A N D R O S K
J E E P B C Y S D D P I
A I J F A D U H Y N E R
C L K I Z E V I R A C T
K M N R X S W K E R I L
P I N E C O N E S G A A
I O D N U O R G I N L N
N P A X D R S T N I P D
E S E E D S A Q K Z O W
R L D G H C S B M A N A
E W L Q E U I O P M M R
F Z X A A C Y T U A E B
S E R O T I N O U S L L
A F A L L Q W H I J K E
I R O N O R E G F E D R
H U N I Q U E U L G C B
P I N E N E E D L E S A
```

Words:

AMAZING
BEAUTY
FALL
FIRE
GLUE
GRAND
GROUND
HEAT

HIKE
IRON ORE
JACK PINE
KIRTLAND WARBLER
LAND
PINE CONES
PINE NEEDLES
RESIN

SEEDS
SEEP
SEROTINOUS
SPECIAL
TALL
UNIQUE

About the Author:

Patricia A. Lin (B.Sc., B.Ed., M.Ed.) is an educator in Calgary, Alberta, Canada, where she resides with her husband, daughter, and dog. When she is not working or writing, she loves spending time out in nature with her family. She is passionate about topics related to nature and the preservation of the Earth.

About the Illustrator:

Victoria A. Kitsco, a retired teacher with a B.A. and a professional diploma in Education, resides in Edmonton, Alberta, Canada. She has enjoyed art all of her life. She is also an avid gardener and a talented pianist. When she is not gardening or doing art, she loves to spend time with her family, including her granddaughter.

Please note:

The author can be contacted at plinauthor@gmail.com
The artist can be contacted at VickyArtist70@gmail.com

If you enjoyed this picture book, you may also enjoy these books, written by the same author:

Incredible Trees
A Mother's Love
Amazing Oceans
Brilliant Skies

You may also want to check out P.A. Lin's Awesome A-Z Nature Word Searches.

Remember to consider posting a review on Amazon if you enjoyed the book!

Namaste ☺